I0828016

IMAGES
of America

BAXTER STATE PARK AND THE ALLAGASH RIVER

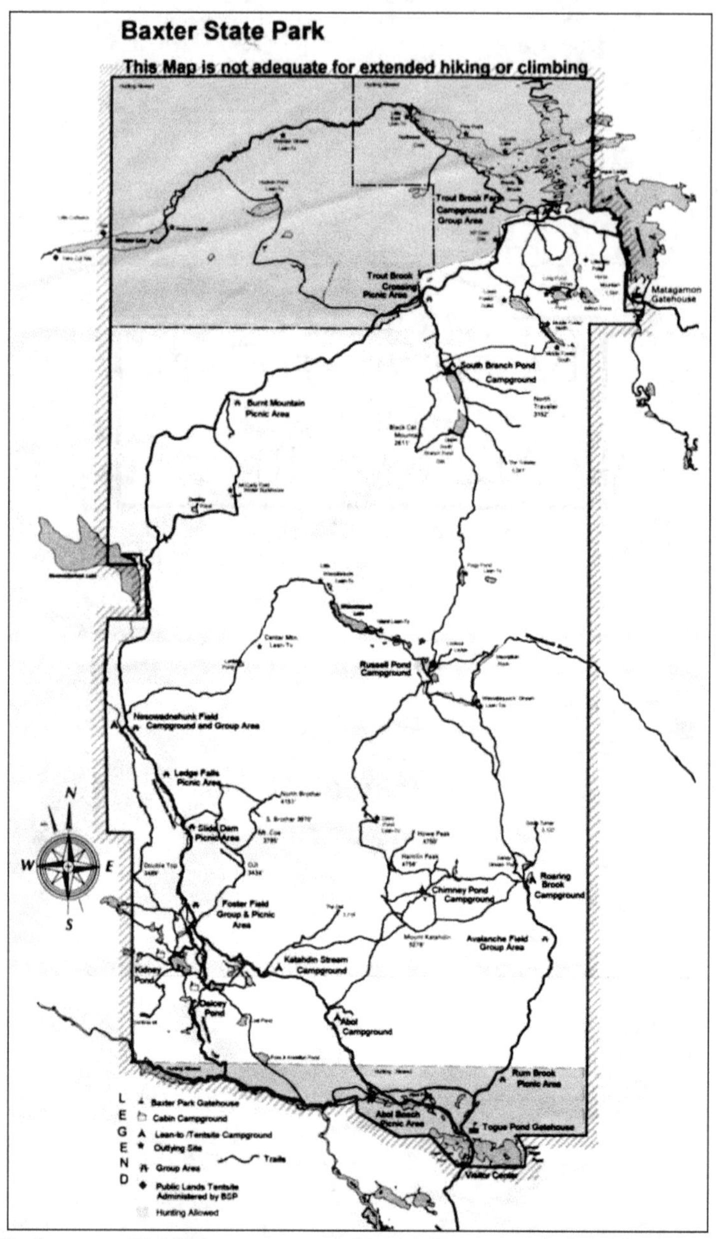

Baxter State Park—now 204,733 acres in northern Maine—includes 46 mountain peaks and ridges; 18 of those peaks are over 3,000 feet high. Except for Mount Katahdin, the northern terminus of the Appalachian Trail, these peaks are often ignored by campers and climbers. There are 10 campgrounds in the park and a gaggle of facilities in those areas. Preserved and put together by former Maine Gov. Percival P. Baxter over about 30 years (not without great difficulty at times), the park was saved from clear cutting—a practice that is becoming less common in the state. Logging is allowed in only a couple of small park areas, one of which was allotted for scientific forestry practices by Governor Baxter. The author had the honor of writing the story, a front-pager in the *Portland Sunday Telegram*, when Governor Baxter made his last acquisition in the park. The author has also climbed Katahdin eight times. Others have climbed it many more times.

IMAGES
of America

Baxter State Park and the Allagash River

Frank H. Sleeper

Copyright © 2002 by Frank H. Sleeper
ISBN 978-1-5316-0627-5

Published by Arcadia Publishing
Charleston, South Carolina

Library of Congress Catalog Card Number: 2001099150

For all general information contact Arcadia Publishing at:
Telephone 843-853-2070
Fax 843-853-0044
E-mail sales@arcadiapublishing.com
For customer service and orders:
Toll-Free 1-888-313-2665

Visit us on the Internet at www.arcadiapublishing.com

Mount Katahdin shows off its winter splendor. It is easy to understand why winter visits to Maine's highest mountain are becoming more popular. It is also easy to understand why the mountain was sacred to Native Americans in the area. While he did not make the climb in the winter, Henry David Thoreau was amongst the many who enjoyed this beautiful area.

Contents

ACKNOWLEDGMENTS

One way or another, this project has been ongoing for 14 years. At that time, Buzz Caverly lent the author the pictures that make up the Kidney Pond camps chapter of this book. Stan and Jackie Greaves of Presque Isle gave the leads that brought many of the pictures in the chapter focusing on the people of the Allagash.

Once again, Earle Shettleworth, executive director of the Maine Historic Preservation Commission, came up with a crucial set of photographs, possibly the oldest ever taken of Mount Katahdin. Vital photographs were also supplied by Marcia Pond-Anderson, curator of the Lumbermen's Museum in Patten. The author was led to her by Ed Rogers, a grandson of the founder of the Lumbermen's Museum, Lore Rogers, and Elliott Hersey, who appeared as a tot in the author's history of Winchester, Massachusetts, which was published by Arcadia.

Robert and Richard Putnam (now both of Ohio) have lent photographs for 14 years; their images of the Allagash appear in this volume. Craig and Terry Hill of Shin Pond Village lent many of the shots that make up the fourth chapter. Bill Greaves, district forest ranger out of the Island Falls district, led the author to the Hills and kept him from putting a photograph in the book that did not belong there. David Putnam, lecturer in science at the University of Maine at Presque Isle, was very helpful. So was Dean Bennett, author of *The Wilderness from Chamberlain Farm*.

In conclusion, thanks go to the author's son, F. Bruce Sleeper, an attorney in Portland, for his last-minute efforts on this book. It should also be made clear that Buzz Caverly and Bob and Dick Putnam will have their photographs by now, photographs that the author held for 14 years.

Dedicated to former Gov. Percival P. Baxter, who fought the good fight and won, and to Irvin C. "Buzz" Caverly Jr., the Cornville diplomat who has flourished as park director.

INTRODUCTION

More than 100,000 people visit Baxter State Park and the Allagash Wilderness Waterway annually. Two thirds of them go to the park; the rest canoe the Allagash. They line up in Millinocket on the first of January to try and get the best locations at the best times in the park. It is hard to judge what former Gov. Percival P. Baxter would have thought about this. He certainly would have felt he did the right thing by creating a park that would remain forever wild. That rightness has also raised cries from people in the area who hate to see camps razed or access cut down or made more difficult.

Here is where Buzz Caverly Jr., the present park director, comes in. All diplomats do not come from Cornville, but this one did. Diplomacy did not solve all problems, however, and Buzz has had to take his share of slurs, slams, and just plain nasty words over the years. As a result, he has acquired a thick skin. You could not find a better fellow for the job.

Why, after all these favorable words, are there no photographs of either Governor Baxter or Buzz Caverly in this volume? In the case of the governor, many photographs of him have been used in other publications. The author hoped to discover the photographs of Arthur Rogers, who probably took more shots of the governor, especially in the Mount Katahdin area, than anyone. However, the reports indicated that time had taken its toll on nearly all of the photographs. I feel the governor would look with approval at this effort to preserve pictures of the area he loved.

And what about Buzz Caverly? In 1960, Caverly was already climbing the ladder to become park director, but he was not yet in that post. The author had word that others were working on books about him, which is why there are no photographs included.

Let us now turn to what is explored in this history. There are two trips, one of which is up Mount Katahdin with photographer A.L. Hinds of Benton. Remember that Henry David Thoreau climbed the mountain late in the summer of 1846. Hinds's photographs were taken a little over 25 years later. They are certainly some of the first photographs ever taken of the mountain. The collection is located in the Augusta headquarters of the Maine Historic Preservation Commission. Do not look for any great differences from the way the mountain looks now. As Governor Baxter pointed out, Mount Katahdin is changeless, which is a reason why he thought the wilderness around it should be preserved.

The second trip is through the Allagash area in the summer of 1946 by Ervin E. "Mike" Putnam and his son, Robert. Some of the area the two covered was within the present Allagash Wilderness Waterway. Some of it is outside the waterway but is certainly part of what was then known as the Allagash in those days. Over the past 56 years, there have been great changes in the Allagash, many of them involving logging roads and access to both the region and, unfortunately, the waterway.

While Buzz Caverly is cutting down on access to Baxter State Park and eliminating camps that have either passed their use or have become somewhat dangerous, the Allagash Wilderness Waterway has not been able to preserve its complete sense of wilderness. Unfortunately, you cannot see the changes in the 1946 photographs, but you can look at those photographs and then make an Allagash trip yourself. Just compare what you see in the 92-mile-long waterway with the photographs presented here.

Also seen is the Mount Katahdin region more recently. Some images, for example, show loggers at work in what is now the park area. Some of the cutting practices in those days were pretty horrible. Governor Baxter had a series of what can only be called fights with pulp and paper companies in the area as he moved to acquire land for the park, a good part of which was on land owned by those companies and by logging firms.

The saga of Kidney Pond Camps in the park unfolds. Started in 1902 by the Hunt brothers, it was officially taken over by the Baxter State Park Authority at the end of 1987. Many of the facilities, including flush toilets, were removed at that time. There is no electricity or running water in the cabins now. It was a turn toward the wilderness experience that Governor Baxter wanted, but it caused considerable controversy at the time. This is another time when Buzz Caverly's diplomacy, combined with his thick skin, worked things out. There is no controversy about Kidney Pond Camps now.

Around the edges of Baxter State Park are places with names like Ripogenus, Chesuncook, and Shin Pond. Chesuncook used to be the starting point for many visitors who traveled around the Allagash River. It was a time of canoe carries to reach the river from the lake. Also view the park area from Shin Pond, which lies to the east.

Moving to the Allagash River, we find ourselves looking at a few of the region's more noted people. They include Al and Patty Nugent of Nugent's Camps; Fred King, who was a guide in the area and had a campsite named after him; Wilfred "Sleepy" Atkins, Allagash guide, game warden, and sporting camp owner; Percy Jackson, who became a river guide at the age of 12; and Ira McNally, a guide for many years in the area. In the final chapter, we take another look at the Allagash. Many of the photographs in this last chapter were taken in the first 20 years of the 1900s.

This is not an all-inclusive history of Baxter State Park and the Allagash River. It is, however, a more thorough pictorial history of the areas than has ever been completed. Arcadia Publishing's *Images of America* series helps popularize history by bringing it to a community or area level. It serves to make public photographs that have never before been published. This book, it is hoped, does just that.

One

Mount Katahdin in the 1870s

Photographer A.L. Hinds listed this image as "Katahdin from Aboljacarmegus Stream." One must assume he meant what is now known as Abol Stream. That certainly looks like Abol Slide on the mountain. The technical difficulty of taking long-range pictures in the early 1870s may have cut down on the quality of the mountain views. Or, it may have been the mighty guardian of Mount Katahdin, Pamola—half-eagle, half-human—who brought poor weather conditions as he sought to preserve his privacy.

This view is on Avalanche Brook, looking up. It was taken three miles from Mount Katahdin, with a group of excursionists. The photograph is by John Bryson of Houlton, shire town of Aroostook County. Many residents of the county enjoyed climbing Mount Katahdin. Bryson originally came from the Canadian province of New Brunswick, just across the border from Houlton.

A camp was set up at the bottom at the foot of the slide (probably Abol Slide), which was one of the ways up to the summit but was usually taken while traveling down the mountain. This is one of the stereo views taken in the early 1870s by A.L. Hinds. The lean-tos in the park are much better constructed than the one shown.

Seen here is a better-defined shot of Mount Katahdin from what Hinds calls "Katepskonegan Lake." Photographers seem to have tested themselves often by taking such long-range shots of the mountain with a lake in the foreground and people in canoes or boats on the lake.

A trapper's home stands in the Baxter Park area *c.* the early 1870s. Cabins in the park now are far superior to this one, although they have no electricity or water. There are still a good number of trappers in Maine. However, they are not allowed to operate in Baxter State Park.

"By the Swan's Road to Katahdin" was the title A.L. Hinds gave to this photograph. Seen is the Penobscot River. The image shows that going to Mount Katahdin was popular among outdoorsmen in the early 1870s.

You will not see this in Baxter State Park today. This appears to be a clear-cutting logging operation, with Mount Katahdin in the background. The photograph was given as a premium to advance paying subscribers to the *Katahdin Kalendar*, published weekly in Sherman. Sherman, now Sherman Mills and Sherman Station, is one of the Aroostook County towns close to Baxter State Park.

Photographer A.L. Hinds called this picture "The Palace of the Pioneer." Note the two children by the right corner of the home. Construction looks quite good, especially for the early 1870s. Except for the roof, such construction might be acceptable even today. Where is the door?

Camping at the foot of the slide in the early 1870s was different than it is today. These men look relatively comfortable in their lean-to. Either it is quite warm or there is a warming fire nearby. Everyone has a hat on to protect against the black flies. Wrappings around the necks of some serve the same purpose.

Excursionists sit on rocks at Katahdin Lake in this early-1870s photograph by John Bryson. The view was taken from the old dam at the lake's outlet. Katahdin Lake lies just to the east of Baxter State Park. It is an unusual photograph, especially in those days.

This photograph of the top of the Abol Slide was taken by A.L. Hinds. The stones may be a little more worn today than they were in the early 1870s. There are now trail markers that did not exist then, but there is still the rocky ruggedness of Katahdin above tree level.

Mount Katahdin is seen from Aboljacarmegus Falls. This is one of A.L. Hinds's better long-range views of the mountain. It must have been a clear day in the spring or fall. Note the snow in the foreground, the ice beginning to form, and the snow on the mountain.

The tableland on the mountain was the place where caribou once grazed. Two unsuccessful attempts were made in the last half of the 20th century to restore the caribou herd. The plateau is down just a bit and is close to the summit of Katahdin. This is an A.L. Hinds photograph.

This is John Bryson's view of the tableland. After you reach Baxter Peak by another trail, the tableland now gives you a respite if you are going down the mountain that way. Bryson calls the tableland the southwestern spur of the mountain. He said the image is looking southwest from Excelsior Peak, which is probably Baxter Peak.

A snowy Mount Katahdin shows up through the fog. This is at the foot of the southwest wall. Winter climbing and camping in Baxter State Park is becoming more and more popular. Special safety regulations are in force for such activities.

Seen here is the dominating summit of Mount Katahdin in the early 1870s. It is now Baxter Peak but was sometimes referred to as Excelsior Peak. Remember that these photographs were taken only about 25 years after Henry David Thoreau climbed to the summit. The top of Mount Katahdin has more traces of civilization on it now than it did then.

A.L. Hinds titled this photograph "View from Eastern Monument—Looking West." What it emphasizes is the mountain's ruggedness. You can jump or climb from boulder to boulder. The author has seen climbers start with full tennis shoes and end with practically nothing on their feet, the shoes torn to shreds on the rocks.

This is one of A.L. Hinds's best Katahdin photographs. It shows what he calls the Sowadnehunk Mountains from Katahdin. Katahdin has overshadowed all other mountains in Baxter State Park. The mountains in the image are gray and seem somewhat foggy, but at least five different peaks can be seen.

Hinds called this photograph "Gorge Looking down toward the Lake Basin." The lake he referred to was probably Chimney Pond. Again is seen the ruggedness of Mount Katahdin. Many feared the mountain, as they believed it was inhabited by the spirit Pamola. Pamola was considered the source of many of the mountain's storms.

Thousands of photographs have been taken of climbers atop Mount Katahdin. This, a premium given to subscribers to the *Katahdin Kalendar,* is certainly one of the earliest photographs ever taken of a group at the summit. These gentlemen seem proud of their accomplishment.

"The Sierra Cliffs across the Lake Basin" was what A.L. Hinds called this photograph. It appears to have been taken from a high point and is included in a section Hinds photographed and titled "The Summit." Regardless of location, it is another example of the grandeur of Katahdin. The cliffs are quite a climb.

Hidden by brook and trees is the northwest wall of Mount Katahdin. This wall is a part of the sheer rise above Chimney Pond. Hinds apparently did not know the name of the brook. In fact, some brooks in the area might not have been named by the early 1870s.

In this view, which was probably taken from Chimney Pond, the northern wall of Mount Katahdin is shown. The mountain, seen from Chimney, Kidney, and Daicy Ponds, is an impressive sight. This Hinds view gives the feel of the magnificence of the mountain.

Seen here is the eastern wall of the basin that rises from Chimney Pond. Hinds apparently took this photograph from high on the mountain. His photographs come from different locations—some from Chimney Pond, others from much higher areas, and some from the summit. He obviously loved the sight of the basin.

The southeastern wall of Mount Katahdin highlights the wild cragginess of the cliffs. This is a good test for the most experienced climbers. It is also part of the magnificent view of the mountain from Chimney Pond. This view has to be experienced to be fully appreciated. The cragginess helps express the power and strength of the mountain.

On a clear day, you can see 30 miles of lakes, streams, and forest from Mount Katahdin. Apparently, Hinds and the photographic equipment of the early 1870s had difficulty getting good photographs of that long view, but at least he made the attempt.

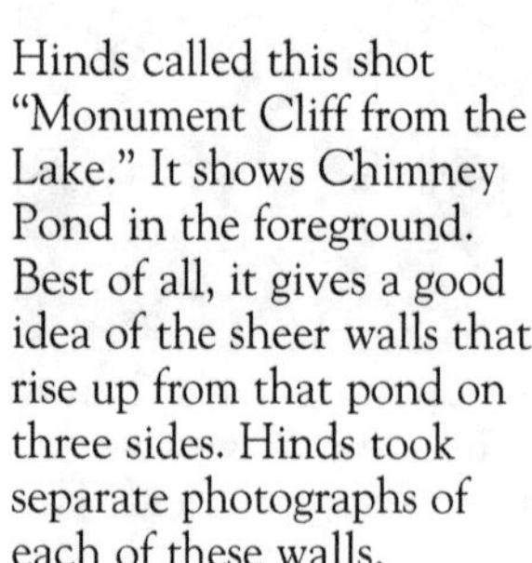

Hinds called this shot "Monument Cliff from the Lake." It shows Chimney Pond in the foreground. Best of all, it gives a good idea of the sheer walls that rise up from that pond on three sides. Hinds took separate photographs of each of these walls.

Houlton photographer John Bryson said this view, looking north from Excelsior Peak, is of the basin and lake (Chimney Pond) at the bottom, with Chase Mountain in the distance. All of Chimney Pond is not visible. Note the heavy growth in the area by the pond.

According to Bryson, this view looks east-northeast from Excelsior Peak and shows the eastern peak and the Chimney's steep area (now a trail for the best climbers), with Katahdin Lake in the distance. It looks suspiciously like the Knife Edge, but Bryson did not mention it. The Knife Edge is not as dangerous as some make it seem, especially when the weather is good.

This view shows you the western peak, second in height, looking west from Excelsior Peak, according to John Bryson. It is apparent that this is not Baxter Peak, which is the highest point on Maine's highest mountain. Note once again how rugged and craggy Katahdin is. Imagine being up there with no trails or trail markings.

Hinds called this photograph "Running Water," but there is more to it than that. Note the rock formation. For an outdoor type, say a Native American or white hunter, it could be a shrine, a place to worship the god of the outdoors. It is no wonder the areas around and on the mountain were sacred to Native Americans.

Two

THE BAXTER STATE PARK AREA MORE RECENTLY

Daicey Dam on the Wassataquoik Stream is shown after the fire of 1884. Logs set adrift from the landing soon pile up on the shore. Such logs, known as rear, made up nine tenths of the work of a river driver. The area in Baxter State Park looks entirely different now.

George Finch's log landing was probably located on Trout Brook, now in Baxter State Park. George Purvis is seen on the far left, and Finch is second from the left. The negative was made by James K. Osgood of Osgood the Jeweler in Houlton. This is one example of what Gov. Percival P. Baxter saved the area from.

A yard of spruce logs rests on Pogey Mountain near Wassataquoik in today's Baxter State Park. The photograph was taken by Lore A. Rogers, founder of the Lumbermen's Museum in Patten. The yard earned money for the loggers that put it together. To most conservationists now, it would only be an eyesore.

The B.W. Howe lumbering operation worked at Trout Brook, now part of the park, in 1901. Fifteen-year-old Frank "Bungie" McElroy (he looks much older) is holding a horse called Knight. In the background is a group of teenagers hamming it up, with two in fighting poses.

Lunch hour does not last long enough for a logging crew on Pogey Mountain, now part of Baxter State Park. There is no sight of the wangan wagon, but the crew is really digging into the food, which often consisted of baked beans and coffee. This photograph is by E.P. Draper.

This is a good action photograph as a team hauls a load of logs at Pogey Mountain, now part of Baxter State Park. It is on a downgrade. With this hauler, the back end drops on the road while the front end is raised on a flat base built up to hold the front end up.

Three logging teams and teamsters pose at Sourdnahunk in what is now Baxter State Park. Among the men are Jud Rigby, Elmer Lord, and Herbert Campbell. These lumbermen were part of a cycle in northern Maine best explored in Dean Bennett's book *The Wilderness from Chamberlain Farm*. Governor Baxter was far ahead of his time in getting started on forming Baxter State Park.

The cook room was, of course, very popular at a lumber camp on Hastings Brook. Seen in this 1917 photograph are, from left to right, Irving Bates, a clerk; unidentified; unidentified; Dave Downing, a cook; and Fred Brown, a teamster. In the tradition of lumber camps, the men ate well. They almost had to because of their exertions in the woods. Note this is only about three years before Governor Baxter began to think seriously about legislation for a park in this area.

A logging camp cook sits on his stool. He looks as though he ate enough of his own food to keep in good shape. With his big handlebar mustache, he looks like someone you would not want to meet in a dark alley. There are a stove and cooking pots behind him.

Between 1900 and 1910, a Finch's or Lawler Brothers crew stands for a photograph with snowshoes and a peavey. Wesley McIntosh (front row, third from left) operated a flume and a raft winch on Grand Lake Matagamon, possibly in the northeastern part of what is now Baxter State Park. Seen with the snowshoes is Bob Hovey from Glassville, New Brunswick. McIntosh was also from New Brunswick. There was a great deal of Canadian influence in northern Maine logging.

The C. Murphy and Son landing was located on Sourdnahunk Stream in 1910, which is in the present park area. The Murphy firm was one of the leading lumbering outfits in the area. Use of the stream for log driving is prohibited now as it is all over the state. Here, the logs show some organization and blend in better with the landscape.

Bam! Off goes the dynamite, and another logjam is broken. Breaking up such jams was one of the most dangerous parts of the logging business. The dynamite often was not enough. Men had to go out on the jam and break it up with their peavies and other equipment. Men were killed quite often doing this. One wonders how many of them died in the area that is now Baxter State Park. This may have been one of the motives behind Governor Baxter's desire to set up the park. It certainly did not encourage any good feelings by him for the logging, pulp, and paper companies, which were strong in their efforts to block the park. Eventually, the governor had better relations with these interests and was able to compromise with them in order to obtain land for the park. Much of what is now parkland has been cut over, and it took years for it to grow back. It continually moves toward the wilderness stage as time goes on.

Logs stand yarded at the head of a sluiceway in the North West Basin of Mount Katahdin. This is a reprint of a photograph by L.A. Rogers that appeared in a 1933 issue of *Appalachia* magazine. This was late fall or winter work on the mountain. It is little wonder that Governor Baxter felt the area should be preserved as a wilderness.

This does not look much like one of the present camp buildings in Baxter State Park. This is an old single camp at Ledge Falls in Sourdnahunk c. 1892. There was no limit in those days to the number of people you could fit in one camp. Nor did there appear to be any limit on the amount of clothing you could hang up to dry.

Here is one more example of just how dangerous log driving could be. These drivers are taking off logs caught on rocks or on gravel bars. Both the areas of the present Baxter State Park and Allagash Wilderness Waterway saw their share of driver injuries and deaths. Imagine the freezing air and water.

Just how tough were the men who logged this area in the late 19th century? Plenty tough. Look at the number here who have no jackets on. Of course, maybe they had three or four layers of shirts. A snub line was another method of holding back a load of logs going downhill.

The log drives that filled the waters of this area in the late 19th and early 20th centuries demanded very hard work from the crews. The logs had to be moved. In this view, there is no snow on the ground, but the water must be cold.

Frank Putnam (front) and his brother Ervin E. "Mike" Putnam stand atop Mount Katahdin in the 1920s. It is not known how many times the brothers, both originally from Houlton, climbed the mountain. However, it was a tradition in their family to do so. Their father, Amos Putnam, last climbed Katahdin at the age of 65, when he had to crawl across the Knife Edge.

This is another example of just how rugged Mount Katahdin is. This man seems comfortable as he gazes into the chasm. He must have been an excellent climber.

Seen here is a view from Mount Katahdin in August 1953. This is one of the eight trips the author made up and down the mountain. A cousin, Robert Putnam, of Marietta, Ohio, has done it 22 times. The author has given up trying to catch up.

By 1953, the cabins at Baxter State Park had improved greatly over those in the late 19th century. This cabin was probably located at Chimney Pond. It is assumed this was a park ranger's cabin.

Katahdin looked like this, probably from Togue Pond, in August 1953. The view has not changed a bit. The timelessness of Mount Katahdin is one of its greatest attributes. Togue Pond had private camps when this photograph was taken. Now, they belong to the Baxter State Park Authority. The photograph was taken by the author's mother.

Here is a good shot of what appears to be the Knife Edge on the mountain. Note the chasm on the left side and the mountain wall on the right. It has often been written about as a dangerous spot. High winds make it very interesting, as does heavy rain.

A much younger author points at the mountain in 1953. That could be Togue Pond. The trees make it unlikely that it is Chimney Pond. This view of the mountain looks like a long-range shot that is similar to the view from Chimney Pond.

In this 1953 view, the author is in the vicinity of Baxter Peak. Note the look of exultation on the face. It does not make any difference how many times one goes up Katahdin. On a warm day like this, one gets dry and can find pools of water in the rocks. The author, somewhere along the line of his eight trips up and down, began to feel the mountain was a friend. That was in spite of having climbed in heavy rain, having gone up on days when the black flies were very thick, and having slept in the open air there.

Dr. Clifton T. Perkins, a Bates College graduate who later became commissioner of mental health in Massachusetts and Maryland, stands on one of the rugged spurs on Katahdin. Climbing the mountain helps one's mental health. You feel invigorated, full of clean air, and a victor because you have reached the summit. There is also peace and quiet in much of the rest of Baxter State Park. This is one of the reasons for the great attraction of the park. It is an excellent place to recuperate both physically and mentally. The scenery, sunrises, and sunsets are spectacular.

John R. Hall of Houlton guided this group of Ricker Classical Institute students and their advisors up Mount Katahdin in the 1930s. The expeditions ended with World War II. Herbert Peabody is the boy with the white sweatshirt and black suspenders. The brave fellows are on a rock that many climbers ascend.

The same group of Ricker students stops for a rest on the mountain. Ricker was in Houlton, the shire town of Aroostook County and a hotbed for Katahdin climbers. John Hall, who guided the Ricker tours, became a close friend of the legendary Roy Dudley. Hall took his family on at least four occasions to hear Dudley, whose cabin was at Chimney Pond, talk about the mountain's folklore.

John Hall is the gentleman in front with the felt hat on. He was a top official of the Bangor and Aroostook Railroad. Hall was an avid outdoorsman all his life. He convinced many of the Ricker students to cross the Knife Edge. He was greatly interested in obtaining publicity for the area.

Ten-year-old Jackie Hall (now Greaves) points to an interesting spot on the mountain, perhaps Pamola Peak. With her is her friend Mary Shaw. John Hall's daughter Jackie recalls returning from the climb to Roaring Brook, then only a wide place in the dirt road where cars were parked, to find her father's car had two flat tires. It was raining, but everyone laughed it off. They did not want to leave the spirit of the mountain.

Seen here is Mount Katahdin from Kidney Pond. The pond is a quiet and restful place where loons are seen. Today, there is no diving board in the center of the pond as there was when this photograph was taken, which was no later than the 1920s.

Hunter Charles W. Parson (left) and his guide, Elmer Hale, pose in the woods near Kidney Pond in 1900. Were they successful when they set off after the posing was over? Today, there is no hunting in the park.

Three

The Kidney Pond Camps

These are Bradeen and Clifford's Camps on Kidney Pond (now Kidney Pond Camps) in the early 1920s. Trails for hiking and climbing extended in all directions. Some went to the many ponds in the area, most of which provided excellent fishing. As detailed in Dean Bennett's book *The Wilderness from Chamberlain Farm*, recreation was the second economic development of the area.

Irving and Lyman Hunt started Kidney Pond Camps in 1902. They were operated privately until 1987, when the Baxter State Park Authority took them over completely, removing many of the amenities such as flush toilets and electric lighting. This photograph shows how camping might have been done in the area before the sporting camps were started.

Seen here is how a Kidney Pond cabin looks now. The lack of electricity (lamps are used) and flush toilets (there are outhouses or backhouses) does not seem to have slowed desire to use the cabins one bit. Demand is almost inelastic.

Hugh N. Knickerbocker came to Kidney Pond Camps in 1910, where he lived until his death in 1960. He died at the age of 91. He helped maintain the hiking trails that fanned out from the camps. On September 17, 1944, Knickerbocker and John Winthrop Worthington (a Harvard Law School–educated Boston lawyer who started coming to the camps when he was 70) climbed Doubletop Mountain, which was four miles from Katahdin. They had Christmas cards made of the handshake by the two atop the mountain.

Here is another 1920s photograph of the Kidney Pond Camp cabins when they were Bradeen and Clifford Camps. Note that the exterior is much like the camps are today. These camps were probably built when Irving Hunt was their active owner, from 1902 to the very early 1920s.

The word *restroom* means one thing now. However, in the 1920s at Kidney Pond Camps, the rest room was a place where you actually rested. And you could do it with music, as the phonograph on the left shows. The camps were then a long way from Governor Baxter's "forever wild" concept.

When it was decided late in 1987 to take modern amenities from Kidney Pond Camps, one argument in favor of doing so was that the camps were too elitist. This photograph of the dining room and rest room at the camps may illustrate just how far from the governor's concept the camps had gone.

Mr. Wells of Boston poses in the woods near the Kidney Pond Camps area in 1900. Of course, the camps did not yet exist. However, not far away on Colt Point, which jutted into Kidney Pond, the Colt family had its private camps. That is a potent gun Wells has over his shoulder. Did he stay with the Colts who were descended from Samuel Colt, inventor of the Colt pistol? Regardless, the Colt establishment became a splendid place after Ethel Barrymore married one of the Colts. Two bowling alleys were placed there because Ethel liked to bowl. John and Lionel Barrymore went there often, possibly to partake of the contents of the wine cellar, heavily weighed in favor of champagne. It is not known if Wells was a partaker or not—but there was prohibition in Maine. The Barrymores evaded it.

Daisy R. Parson, booted and rifle in hand, hangs out in the woods near Kidney Pond in 1900. She does not appear to be dressed for either the occasion or the black flies. Perhaps she was impervious to the latter. The look on her face indicates that she was.

The cabin on the left belonged to Colonel Colt at the Colt complex on Kidney Pond in 1912. It takes a little imagination to see the Barrymores there. The complex was started in 1885. It ended up with a grand piano, English china, Waterford crystal, and sterling silver with the Colt crest on it.

Advertisements from *In the Maine Woods*, the Bangor and Aroostook Railroad publication, give us a good idea of what the Kidney Pond Camps were like. Dick Sprague, then the railroad's public relations chief, allowed the author to use material from that magazine years ago. This 1909 advertisement maps the location, calls it "Hunt's territory," and shows the Hunt Trail up Mount Katahdin, which Irving Hunt blazed.

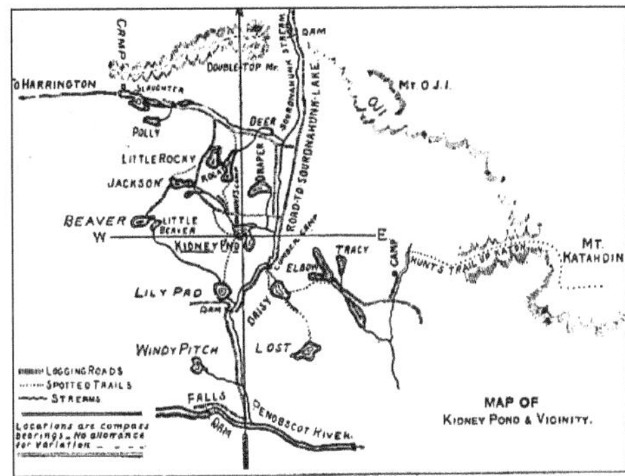

Here's Our Stamping Ground

THE map shows Hunt's territory. There is no better in the state for fishing, for hunting, or simply to spend your outing there surrounded by all the good things of camp life. Easy to get to by a delightful trip up the beautiful West branch of the Penobscot to the mouth of Sourdnahunk Stream and up the stream three miles to Kidney Pond. Here is some of the finest scenery to be found in the state. Twenty-three ponds handy to the home camp offer unequalled trout fishing all summer. A special feature this year is the Harrington Lake fishing trip. The camp is right in the heart of the great Sourdnahunk moose region. Hunt's trail up Mt. Katahdin starts at the camp and a five hour trip takes one to the top of the mountain. This is the favorite starting point for the climb, the best trail, and a camp on the mountain side. The accommodations here are unsurpassed anywhere. Cosy camps, the best of beds, and the best of table fare. Fresh vegetables from our own garden, fresh eggs, fresh milk and butter. The purest spring water and a large ice house are on the premises. Good canoes and experienced guides furnished. NO PLACE IN MAINE CAN YOU GET SUCH A VARIETY OF GOOD SIDE TRIPS AS HERE.

For detailed information write to or telegraph,

I. O. HUNT, (P. O.) Kidney Pond, Maine

The advertisement format changed in 1913. It became "I.O. Hunt's Famous Camps." Once again, the 23 ponds in the area are stressed. The camps are "close by Mount Katahdin which can be climbed by our own trail." Fresh food is played up. Irving Hunt was certainly not bashful. "No resort in the Maine woods offers greater attractions," his advertisement declares.

Change came again in 1918. Hunt went into partnership with a man named Bradeen from nearby Millinocket (Hunt lived in Hampden). It therefore became "Hunt & Bradeen." Otherwise, the advertisement remained the same. Vegetables still came from the camp garden, and there was fresh butter, milk, and eggs.

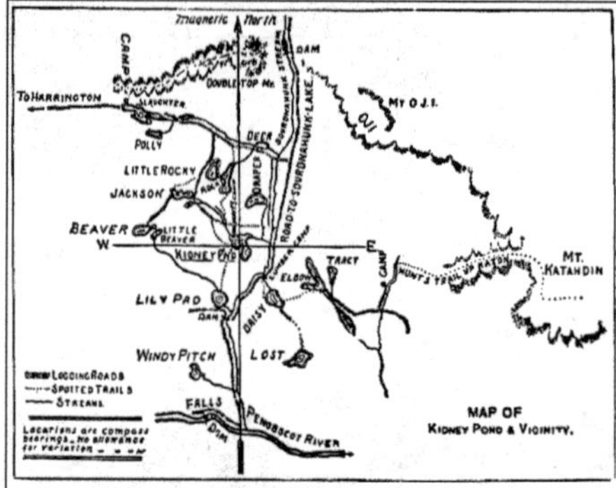

By 1921, Irving Hunt was out as an owner of the camps. They had become "Bradeen & Clifford." It is "Kidney Pond Famous Camps, under new management." Added was this: "Our new hunting lodges at Abol and Slaughter Pond are in the midst of one of the best game countries in Maine."

In the 1922 Bradeen & Clifford advertisement, this addition is noted: "Auto parties can store their cars at Ripogenus Dam, go down the river on the left side to the big eddy, or take the better road on the right side and cross at the eddy to the direct trail to our camps at Kidney Pond." Rates at the camps were $4 a day, $24.50 a week, and $90 per month.

MAP OF KIDNEY POND & VICINITY

Kidney Pond Famous Camps

UNDER NEW MANAGEMENT

Offer attractions unsurpassed in the Maine Woods. Handy to 23 ponds—all famous for fishing; close by Mt. Katahdin, which can be climbed by our own trail; in a section renowned for big game and trout fishing. Table Fare of First Quality—vegetables from our own garden, fresh butter, milk and eggs; in fact, everything is of the high-class order that you'd expect at this justly celebrated woods resort.

Reach by the way of Norcross, Me.

No Resort in the Maine Woods Offers Greater Attractions

Auto parties can store their cars at Ripogenus Dam, go down the river on the left side to the big eddy, or take the better road on the right side and cross at the eddy to the direct trail to our camps at Kidney Pond.

Many Ideal Side Trips for Which We Furnish Canoes and Experienced Guides

Our chief aim is to make your vacation so pleasant for you that each one to come will be spent at Kidney Pond, one of the most beautiful resorts in Maine.

Our new booklet and map tells more about our camps and this choice country. Write for it. We will also be pleased to furnish any information desired, and can furnish the names and addresses of well-known parties who will gladly recommend us. Telephone in camps. Rates $4.00 per day, $24.50 per week, $90.00 per month.

Through Pullman Sleeping Cars between Boston and Norcross.

P. O. Address

BRADEEN & CLIFFORD

NORCROSS MAINE

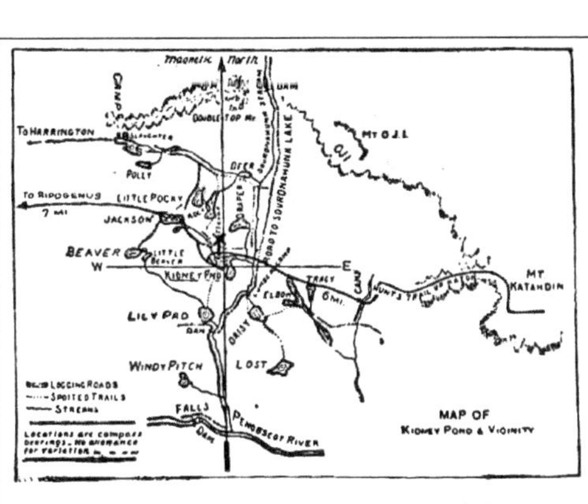

KIDNEY POND FAMOUS CAMPS

Offer attractions unsurpassed in the Maine Woods. Handy to 23 ponds—all famous for fishing, fine stream fishing with plenty of salmon at the river, close by Mt. Katahdin, which can be climbed by our own trail; in a section renowned for big game and all season trout fishing.

Auto parties can drive from Greenville around the shore of Moosehead Lake, across the river at the Great Northern Paper Company's big dam to Sourdnahunk Stream, where our team meets you and takes you to camp. NO WALKING.

Reached by the way of Norcross, Maine, or we will meet you at Greenville or Ripogenus.

NO RESORT IN THE MAINE WOODS OFFERS GREATER ATTRACTIONS

Many ideal side trips for which we furnish canoes and experienced guides

With our large new kitchen and dining-room we will be able to furnish a table fare of first quality with the aid of vegetables, fresh milk and eggs from our own farm, in fact everything will be of the high class order that you would expect at this justly celebrated woods resort.

Fishing season opens May 1, closes Sept. 30
Hunting season opens Oct. 15, closes Nov. 30

Come early for the best fishing

Our chief aim is to make your vacation so pleasant for you that *each one* to come will be spent at Kidney Pond, one of the most beautiful resorts in Maine.

Our new booklet and map tell more about our camps and this choice country. Write for it. We will also be pleased to furnish any information desired, and can furnish the names and addresses of well-known parties who will gladly recommend us. Telephone connection in camps.

Through Pullman Sleeping Cars between Boston and Norcross

Post-office Address

BRADEEN & CLIFFORD

NORCROSS, OR MILLINOCKET - - - - MAINE

In 1924, there were more additions, and the automobile had much to do with them. "Auto parties can drive from Greenville around the shore of Moosehead Lake, across the river at the Great Northern Paper Company's big dam to Sourdnahunk Stream, where our team meets you and takes you to camp. NO WALKING." Trains were not overlooked. "Through Pullman Sleeping Cars between Boston and Norcross," the advertisement says.

Famous Kidney Pond Camps

In the Katahdin Region

The beautiful location of Kidney Pond Camps and their countless advantages make them unsurpassed for enjoyable and healthful recreation. Delightful trails lead in all directions through fragrant woods. Within view and hiking distance are majestic Mt. Katahdin, Mt. Roosevelt, Doubletop, and O. J. I. These mountains provide the climber with ascents of varying difficulty.

In twenty easily accessible ponds the fisherman may hook trout to his heart's content. He may fish streams, too, and the Penobscot River for salmon.

The cabins, all facing the lake, are comfortably furnished and immaculately clean. Exceptionally good food is served, including an abundance of fresh vegetables, milk, and eggs from our own farm. For the greater comfort of hikers, fishermen, and hunters, there are now two outlying camps, one on picturesque Slaughter Pond, the other on the Penobscot River. Adjacent woods are unexcelled for game in the hunting season.

Write early for illustrated booklet and map giving more detailed information. Season, May 10th to December 1st.

Address

BRADEEN & BRADEEN

Kidney Pond Camps - - - Millinocket, Maine

By 1936, Bradeen and Bradeen were the owners. The advertisement was somewhat smaller. The number of "easily accessible ponds" had shrunk to 20. The "two outlying camps" were on Slaughter Pond and the Penobscot River. "Within view and hiking distance are majestic Mount Katahdin, Mount Roosevelt, Doubletop and O.J.I.," it points out.

FAMOUS KIDNEY POND CAMPS

In the Katahdin Region

The beautiful location of Kidney Pond Camps and their countless advantages make them unsurpassed for enjoyable and healthful recreation. Delightful trails lead in all directions through fragrant woods. Within view and hiking distance are majestic Mt. Katahdin, Mt. Roosevelt, Doubletop, and O. J. I. These mountains provide the climber with ascents of varying difficulty.

In twenty easily accessible ponds the fisherman may hook trout to his heart's content. He may fish streams, too, and the Penobscot River for salmon.

The cabins, all facing the lake, are comfortably furnished and immaculately clean. Exceptionally good food is served, including an abundance of fresh vegetables, milk, and eggs from our own farm. For the greater comfort of hikers, fishermen, and hunters, there are now two outlying camps, one on picturesque Slaughter Pond, the other on Penobscot River. Adjacent woods are unexcelled for game in the hunting season.

Write early for illustrated booklet and map giving more detailed information. Season, May 10th to December 1st.

Address

LAURA P. BRADEEN

Kidney Pond Camps Millinocket, Me.

Two years later, the advertisement was much the same except for the ownership name at the bottom. The owner was Laura P. Bradeen, the widow of one of the Bradeens. Apparently, the males had passed away. One change that was made was the addition of "In the Katahdin Region" under the camps' headlined name.

Next year, the ownership name changed to Mrs. Roy Bradeen. She was succeeded by Charles Lipscomb and Charles Norris. Perhaps Bradeen felt that using the name of her husband, who had run the camps before passing away, would draw in more business.

FAMOUS
KIDNEY POND CAMPS
In the Katahdin Region

The beautiful location of Kidney Pond Camps and their countless advantages make them unsurpassed for enjoyable and healthful recreation. Delightful trails lead in all directions through fragrant woods. Within view and hiking distance are majestic Mt. Katahdin, Mt. Roosevelt, Doubletop, and O. J. I. These mountains provide the climber with ascents of varying difficulty.

In twenty easily accessible ponds the fisherman may hook trout to his heart's content. He may fish streams, too, and the Penobscot River for salmon.

The cabins, all facing the lake, are comfortably furnished and immaculately clean. Exceptionally good food is served, including an abundance of fresh vegetables, milk, and eggs from our own farm. For the greater comfort of hikers, fishermen, and hunters, there are now two outlying camps, one on picturesque Slaughter Pond, the other on the Penobscot River. Adjacent woods are unexcelled for game in the hunting season.

Write early for illustrated booklet and map giving more detailed information. Season, May 10th to December 1st.

Address

MRS. ROY BRADEEN

Kidney Pond Camps Millinocket, Maine

Famous 1942

KIDNEY POND CAMPS

in the

KATAHDIN COUNTRY

•

An alluring vacationland which combines simplicity, comfort and good food. Homelike atmosphere. Restricted clientele. American plan. Automobile road 30 miles from Millinocket, 63 miles from Greenville. Excellent fly fishing all through the season for trout in twelve of our ponds. Landlocked salmon fishing down to the West Branch of the Penobscot River. Bathing, canoeing and mountain climbing, also nice clean trails for hiking. Excellent hunting for bear and deer.

A Friendly Place for Nice People

(Mrs.) ROY BRADEEN

BOX 300 MILLINOCKET, MAINE

Telephone and Telegrams via Greenville, Maine

U. S. mail via Millinocket, Maine

Write for Free Booklet

MAKE RESERVATIONS EARLY

This *In the Maine Woods* advertisement was done with a new design in 1942. The advertisement is larger, and the print is blacker. Now we have "an alluring vacationland which combines simplicity, comfort and good food. Homelike atmosphere. Automobile road 30 miles from Millinocket, 63 miles from Greenville. . . . A Friendly Place for Nice People."

You do not see this sign anymore. It apparently went out with other amenities. However, Kidney Pond Camps are still in use, much closer to the "forever wild" concept than they had been from 1902 to 1987. The lack of amenities has not changed and may well have increased the appeal of this spot in Baxter State Park.

Four

AROUND THE EDGES OF BAXTER STATE PARK

John Bryson took this photograph of the Hunt Farm on the East Branch of the Penobscot River with Wassataquoik Mountain in the distance. Bryson spelled it differently, with the letter *i* in place of the first *a*. It is unknown to the author just how well Bryson was acquainted with the Katahdin area, and spellings in that area changed over the years, including that of Katahdin itself.

This boom house stood at Ambajejus (spelled Ambijegis by A.L. Hinds) Lake. The boom was part of log drives on Maine rivers. Such log drives on the rivers are now forbidden. The booms held large amounts of logs. Apparently, these two men had charge of the boom. Ambajejus Lake is just south of Baxter State Park.

In this A.L. Hinds photograph, Ripogenus Lake looms up before there was a dam. Ripogenus Lake is only a few miles west of Baxter State Park. It is also close to Chesuncook Lake, which has been used to start the Allagash canoe trip for years. Ripogenus Lake is larger now.

The Arches at Ripogenus Falls are narrow, as A.L. Hinds had pictured them. This view is close to the Ripogenus Gorge. You will not find logs such as these in the gorge now. The view is now entirely different from that shown in the 1870s. This image helps show the importance of logging in the Katahdin area then.

The head of Ripogenus Falls in the early 1870s no longer looks like this. The Ripogenus dam has changed things. Notice the heavy forest cover on both banks with mixed hardwoods and softwoods. Industry has changed much of this, for better or worse. The better is more hydroelectric power for Maine paper plants.

A logjam blocks the river at Aboljacarmegus Falls. There has been none of this in the state since log river drives were prohibited in the 1970s. Because men often walked out on the jams to break them up, many river drivers were killed in their efforts.

This view from the cliff of Ripogenus Falls shows the Ripogenus Gorge, through which logs were sometimes sent in the 19th century. This was one of the most beautiful scenic sights in Maine. In a way, it is reminiscent of Gulf Hagas, Maine's little Grand Canyon.

A lone canoeist puts out into Chesuncook Lake in the early 1870s. This is the lake just west of Baxter State Park where there was a flourishing village with a hotel in the past. The village is at the northern tip of the lake. The hotel was one of the reasons why Chesuncook Lake was often a starting point for the Allagash canoe trip.

Edwin Rogers, walking boss of a lumber operation and son of lumber operator Luther B. Rogers, stands on snowshoes with a pipe in hand. He personified the well-adjusted lumbermen who operated in the Baxter State Park area in the late 19th and early 20th centuries. Is that money he is carrying in his left hand?

Ezra Robar and his dog are canoeing on Katahdin Lake near the outlet dam *c.* 1896. This photograph, from the Caleb Scribner collection, is almost a standard, with varying individuals in canoes and Mount Katahdin in the background. However, it was not as common at the end of the 19th century. The dog, unfortunately, is unidentified. Governor Baxter, a great dog lover, would not have liked that.

Rodney Barker's steamboat *M.E. Gove* rests on Mattawamkeag Lake in Aroostook County. Built *c.* 1895 by Barker, it was used for towing logs and for excursions. Two steamboats on Chamberlain Lake in the Allagash, the *H.W. Marsh* and *George A. Dugan*, were somewhat similar. They hauled logs and ended up decaying at Chamberlain Farm.

E.T. Spencer's logging camp, shown *c.* 1895, was in West Bog. Replace the horses with machinery, and one can see what Governor Baxter saved the area from. This image is from the Carl Sprinchorn collection. Sprinchorn was an artist who painted, among other things, the area that is now the northern part of Baxter State Park. He spent much time at Shin Pond.

Millinocket Lake is peaceful and calm in this early-1870s photograph by A.L. Hinds. This lake is just outside Baxter State Park, and you pass it on the way to the southern entrance to the park.

A sluiceway works over Shin Brook Falls. There were sluiceways in various spots on Maine rivers and streams to aid logs in going over or around falls or other difficult places for the log drives. Most were very effective. Some were quite long. This one was located east of the present park area. Lumbermen used all sorts of devices to speed up the movement of logs to market. The best known was the Telos Cut (Canal), which diverted the waters of the Allagash south so the logs could get to Bangor more rapidly. A short railway was built in the Allagash area. Its engines still rest peacefully in the woods. A long trestle was built across Chamberlain Lake in the Allagash as part of that railroad. Eventually, roads for pulp and paper trucks took the place of all those embellishments.

This photograph by Ervin E. Putnam shows a moose running on Route 11, then a dirt road, north in the 1920s. Putnam tinted the photograph himself. The location is not too far from the Allagash. This moose had been standing still in the middle of the road. Putnam got out of the car for a photograph, and the moose started running. Putnam got back in the car, the driver got it going, and this was the result.

Moving nearer to Baxter State Park, we come to Shin Pond, east of the park, on its northern entrance road from Patten and Sherman. These are some of the cabins of the Shin Pond Inn, which has an excellent view of the park. Some of these cabins are still in use as part of the Shin Pond Village.

Seen here is Lower Shin Pond. You get some idea of the mostly quiet and peaceful atmosphere of this area from this photograph. However, motors, planes, and trucks give it sounds that are almost never heard in Baxter State Park.

This is the East Branch of the Penobscot River as seen from what was known as the Shin Pond House. That is Mount Chase in the background. The scene is close to the outlet from Upper Shin Pond. Beautiful scenery exists not only in the park and Allagash Wilderness Waterway, but also around the borders of those two areas.

This road is to the northern entrance gate of Baxter State Park. The mountain is Horse Mountain. The image shows how the underpublicized northern area of Baxter State Park is full of scenic splendor. Imagine what the scenery is like when fall foliage is in full bloom.

This is another scenic view of the area east of Baxter State Park. We see the East Branch of the Penobscot River. The water is so low that it must have been summer. The scenery would probably be far better in the early fall. It does not look like good canoeing.

The bridge over the Shin Ponds is seen from Lower Shin Pond. Shin Pond is not a town unto itself. It is part of the town of Mount Chase. Note the many birch trees in the woods. Almost all the area has been cut over in the past.

The Shin Pond House burned several times in the past. On March 3, 1974, its store burned down. On December 7, 1979, Shin Pond House itself burned, and the lodge was vacant for three years. Built in the 1800s, it also burned in 1911, 1912, and 1949. This is a long-range view of the Shin Pond House complex. It was taken sometime before 1919.

The Shin Pond House is on the right. The cabin on the left was moved to Lower Shin Pond in the 1950s after the main building was destroyed by fire in 1949. The people on its front porch certainly look comfortable. Views from that porch must have been excellent.

Built in 1912, this dining room at the Shin Pond House disappeared when the building burned in 1949. There is, of course, a dining area at the present Shin Pond Village. There are varied facilities around Baxter State Park that supply amenities not found in the park.

Here is northern Baxter State Park at its best. The Wassataquoik Valley is in the center, surrounded by mountains. This photograph is another example of the great scenery found in the underpublicized northern area of the park. Mount Katahdin, in the southern part of the park, has overshadowed almost everything else.

Sugarloaf Mountain looms in the background in this image from Lower Shin Pond, near Brown Sand Beach. Again, we are looking toward the park. Sugarloaf (not the ski area mountain) lies between Shin Pond and the park and is outside the park itself. This is great scenery in an often overlooked area.

Here is a cabin at Point of Pines Camps on Upper Shin Pond. These camps are now operated by the Riley family. Again, if you cannot get reservations to stay within the park, you will find facilities just outside it. At most of these facilities, you will also be close to good boating and fishing areas.

This is the Shin Pond House in its prime in 1921. Zene Harvey was the proprietor. This was about the time the automobile was taking over in the area. Obviously, multiple groups have posed for this photograph. The wheels on two of the cars almost look like wagon wheels. The note on the back says, "Do you know this place? Homelike isn't it."

The Hill family was picking berries on Owlsboro Road in Mount Chase when this photograph was taken in the 1920s. Craig and Terry Hill are now the owners of Shin Pond Village, which has campgrounds, cottages, guest suites, country store, snack bar, craft shop, and snowmobile rentals at the site. It is the same location as where the Shin Pond House stood.

Traveler Mountain is another overlooked mountain in the northern part of Baxter State Park. This is Hurricane Deck scenic turnout on Route 159, the Matagamon Road (also called the Traveler Mountain Road). This photograph was taken in the 1920s. Unfortunately, the turnout no longer exists. The Haskell deadwater of the East Branch of the Penobscot River is seen in the left middle of the photograph.

They had their own hay at the Shin Pond House in the 1920s. It was strictly utilitarian. As you see, the hay mows were right behind the cabins. Certainly, the inhabitants of the cabins had no worries—except for those suffering from hay fever.

Shin Pond was also the location of a Civilian Conservation Corps (CCC) camp, as this 1934 photograph shows. The CCC did all kinds of good work in what is now Baxter State Park. Much of that work is still visible and in use. The CCC was certainly one of the most valuable Great Depression aid programs.

One of the most famous salmon fishermen in the state's history, Guy "Daddy" Carroll, originally from Houlton, sits in the Bangor and Aroostook Railroad stop at Griswold in 1915. Carroll made his angling reputation by catching Atlantic salmon in the Bangor Salmon Pool. Some of those fish were sent to the president of the United States as the first catch of the season.

This boy is delivering groceries near Clayton Lake, only a few miles west of the Allagash Wilderness Waterway in northwestern Maine. The dog looks a bit eager. Note the wooden wheels on the cart. The barn in the background does not appear in the best of shape.

Five
An Allagash Trip

In late June 1946, Ervin E. "Mike" Putnam, his son Bob, and a man named Mark Rand took a trip into the area around Allagash Lake and beyond. The senior Putnam considered Allagash Lake the most beautiful lake in Maine. This was the camp at Round Pond, only a short distance from the lake.

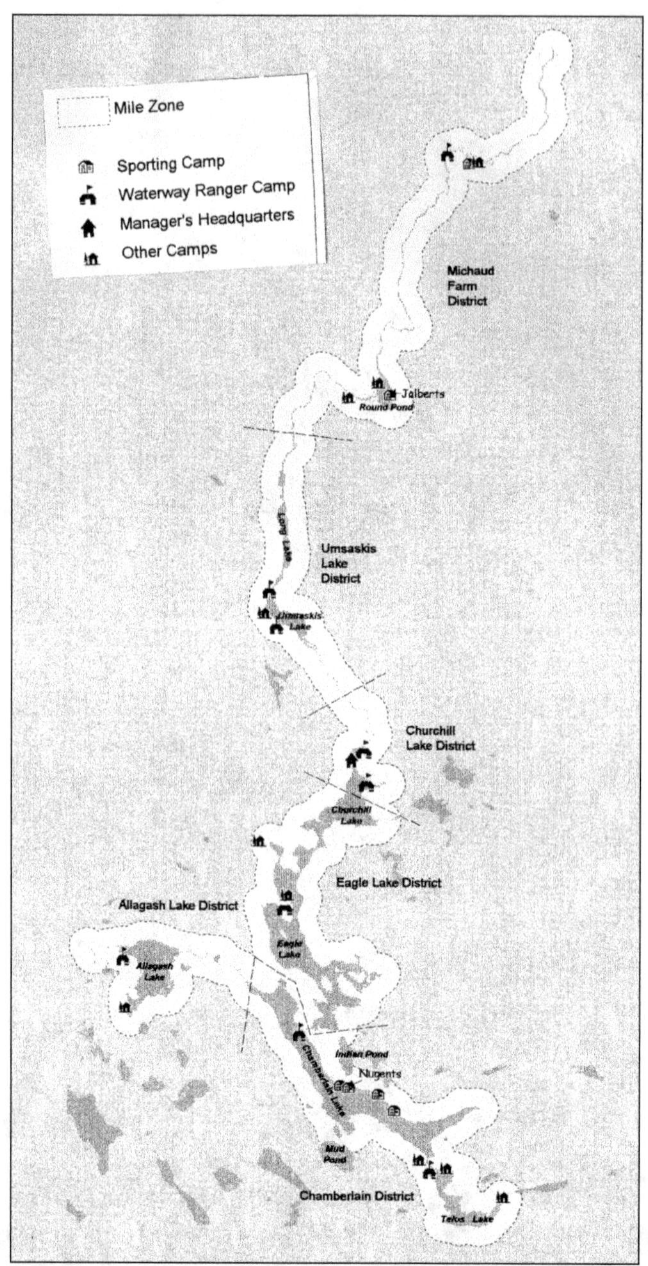

These are the administrative structures and districts along the 92-mile Allagash Wilderness Waterway. Many canoe trips now start at Telos Lake and move north along the river, often branching off to go to Allagash Lake. In the past, the trip often began at Northeast Carry, at the northern tip of Moosehead Lake. Others started at Chesuncook Lake. The opening of roads led to Telos Lake becoming the starting point, but there are all kinds of variations on the canoe trip. The river went through the lumbering era and itself would now be part of that era except for the protective waterway strip. From south to north, the waterway includes Telos Lake, Round Pond, Chamberlain Lake, Eagle Lake, Churchill Lake, Heron Lake, Umsaskis Lake, Long Lake, Harvey Pond, and another Round Pond. Including Allagash Lake and Allagash stream off to the west, the full canoe trip takes 7 to 10 days.

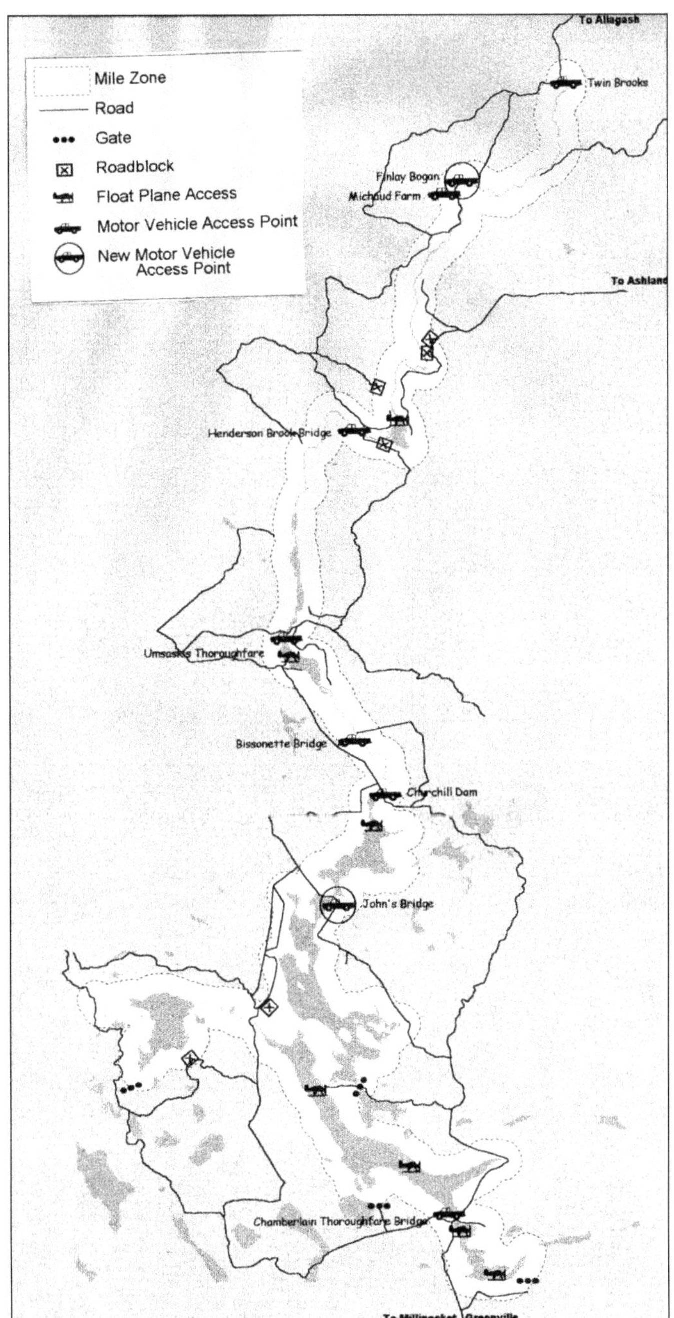

These are access points on the Allagash Wilderness Waterway. According to the Wilderness Society, there are now 12 major access points on the waterway compared to only 4 when it was opened. Many believe the canoe trip is being spoiled as a result. Is the Allagash Wilderness Waterway living up to the expectations of then Sen. Edmund S. Muskie or then Secretary of the Interior Stewart L. Udall, who worked out its inception? Many believe it is not. If it is not, the administration of the waterway may become a prime argument for the specter of a national park that continues to hover over the area. Time alone will tell what happens. Meanwhile, we will take a trip on the Allagash before there was any Allagash Wilderness Waterway.

Caucomgomoc Lake is just southwest of Round Pond but is still close to the present waterway. Canoes are shown at the mouth of Ciss Stream on the lake on June 20, 1946. This image captures the flavor of the Allagash canoe experience.

It is June and these are the Poland Pond Dam Falls of a stream that enters Round Pond. The group shown fishing has caught a lot of good square tail trout. One fisherman in the photograph actually has a trout on his line. Good fishing is part of the Allagash experience.

It is better to have your waders on when you go into the Allagash area. This fisherman knew that well. The stream runs from Poland Pond to Round Pond. June fishing is not always good, but this time it was.

Just how good was the fishing on June 21, 1946, at Poland Pond Stream and dam? Mike Putnam gives an example. You can bet many of those beauties were quickly eaten by the three men. The Allagash is not entirely lakes, ponds, streams, and trees. Note the field in which Putnam stands. Farms were started there. Unfortunately, many were abandoned.

You could travel quite lightly to the Allagash in 1946, but a long canoe on a trailer was essential. On the way from Leeds, Massachusetts, you could pick up other supplies in a town like Greenville at the Sanders store. This photograph of Mike Putnam was taken in Pinkham Notch, New Hampshire, on June 19, 1946.

Seen in this view is the shore of the camp at Allagash Lake where the three men stayed. Welcoming people are at hand in the photograph. The water shows that June 22, 1946, was a calm day.

Ray O'Donnell's plane sits on Allagash Lake in this 1946 photograph. It is more than 20 years before the ban on planes at that lake went into effect. Even then, however, the atmosphere looks quite peaceful.

Canoeing and fishing are not the only activities that take place on an Allagash trip. There are clothes and dishes to wash. Also, you have to hang the clothing out to dry, as these two campers on Allagash Lake have done. The dirty dishes on the low wooden table show that they have eaten. Maybe the two are discussing the big one that got away.

Allagash Lake had plenty of fish. Bob Putnam, sitting in a canoe, shows off two good-sized togue, or lake trout. Fishing may not be quite as good now, but it will do until something else comes along.

It is not quite like home, but it will certainly do when you are on the Allagash. The trio traveled to Chamberlain Lake. The camp where they stayed was at the mouth of Ellis Brook, which runs into that big lake. The camp's location was just across the lake from Chamberlain Dam.

Mark Rand had this tent near the shore of Chamberlain Lake. Again, there are not all the comforts of home, but it is certainly comfortable and peaceful enough for an Allagash journey. Where else can you get air like this, and where else can you get such a setting on a sunny day?

Mike Putnam is applying 448 repellent to combat the bugs swarming on June 23, 1946. The author worked on a *Sports Illustrated* story that featured a blown-up picture of a single black fly, a small creature that can barely be seen. In the enlarged view, it appeared to be a real monster.

Allagash Lake looked great from the camp on a summer day in June 1946. This photograph helps give a small idea of scenery on the Allagash.

"An Allagash Lake Panorama" was the title for this image when it was taken. It was part of the reason why Mike Putnam considered Allagash Lake the most beautiful lake in Maine. We see the mix of softwoods and hardwoods, including spruce and birch. None of this is now being cut and is protected.

Allagash Mountain is part of the excellent scenery around Allagash Lake. You could fly in and even run a motorboat on the lake in 1946, something you have not been able to do since 1970 when the Allagash Wilderness Waterway went into effect. Combine the peace of the lake with scenery like this and you cannot go wrong.

Even if you do not have a canoe, you can fish on Allagash Lake. Bob Putnam casts from the shore on June 24, 1946. There is no record of just what the learned angler caught. You do not see anything in the way of fish lying on the ground.

When water is low in the Allagash area, one often has to pull a canoe up a stream. This is a view of the stream that flows out of Mud Pond. Usually, the water was deeper than this. Mud Pond is located near Chamberlain Lake.

Mike Putnam wipes some of the dinner dishes. The water heats at the fireplace. Clothes are drying on the line. Note the holders hanging above the fireplace. One holds the water heating for the dishes.

There is nothing like fly-fishing on the Allagash. Sitting in a canoe, Mike Putnam has a good togue on his line. In that one day, the trio caught 100 fish on flies.

There are plenty of canoe carry areas in the Allagash. It is good for one's constitution and is not always easy. Seen is one of the spots that required a canoeist to carry his canoe around the falls at Little Allagash Lake. This photograph was taken on June 27, 1946.

In 1946, the 1,500-foot trestle on Chamberlain Lake, part of the 16-mile Chesuncook and Chamberlain Railroad, was still standing but unused. The railroad, open by 1927, operated only until 1933. It ran from the tramway on Eagle Lake to the head of Umbazooksus Lake. It carried large amounts of pulpwood. The Great Depression and low paper-product prices brought its end. The trestle no longer exists.

The father-son team of Mike and Bob Putnam move along in the Allagash. Both were skilled canoeists. Mike Putnam learned from his father, Amos Putnam of Houlton. Bob Putnam, in turn, learned from his father.

Here is more great Allagash scenery. We see Chamberlain Lake on June 27, 1946. In the foreground is a quantity of dri-ki (dead timber killed by flooding). One could think it was the remains of one of the abandoned steamboats in front of Chamberlain Farm, but they were more intact in 1946.

There are dams all over the Allagash. This is the one at Chamberlain Lake. It is certainly not a bad-looking dam as dams go. There are some other dams in the Allagash that add nothing to the scenery but serve a great purpose.

Mike Putnam stands next to an unidentified dam tender at Chamberlain Lake. You wonder about a man living all alone in the small house at the rear. He must love the outdoors and his privacy. There is work being done on the house's roof.

This is a new lake for the group on the Allagash. It is Eagle Lake on June 28, 1946. That lake is just north of Chamberlain Lake on the Allagash Wilderness Waterway. Taken from the canoe, this image shows a lot of water and not much land scenery.

Mike Putnam (left) and Dr. Fred E. Steele, who was on the medical staff at the Veterans Administration Hospital in Northampton, Massachusetts, leave camp at Ellis Brook, which runs into Chamberlain Lake. Putnam was an x-ray technician at the same hospital. That is a 20-foot Old Town canoe, one of the longest ever made by that company.

The entrance to Mud Pond Stream from Chamberlain Lake is very scenic. It is the start of the end of the Allagash-area trip. This is the traditional old-time route for the Allagash trip. There is no sign of mud in this photograph.

The canoe is pulled up at this camp on Umbazooksus Lake. Umbazooksus is southwest of Chamberlain Lake and Mud Pond. It is just outside the Allagash Wilderness Waterway and on the way to Chesuncook Lake. We are going backwards on the route many used to take on the way to the Allagash.

Finally, Ben Gunn's mailboat tows the group's two canoes down Chesuncook Lake on June 30, 1946. Hopefully, the images of this trip have given people a sense of the atmosphere of the Allagash region over 50 years ago.

Six

Allagash People

Nugent's on Chamberlain Lake is shown in its first year of operation in 1937. Al Nugent is probably the man on the right. The previous year, Al and Patty Nugent, along with some helpers, rafted a huge amount of food and equipment across the lake to the spot they had selected as the site of their sporting camps.

As the years progressed, Nugent's became legendary on the Allagash, in the state, and to clients across the nation. Adding to the legend was the main lodge at Nugent's, with its big bobcat skin and trophy fish. With Patty's superb cooking, the great fishing and hunting, and Al "Nuge" Nugent's after-dinner story hour each evening, the camp became very popular. One of the Nugents' best friends was Robert Haskell, the president of the Bangor Hydro-Electric Company. Haskell got them fuel and sugar during early World War II (the couple went to work for Pratt & Whitney in Connecticut the latter part of the war), helped Patty get into a Bangor hospital when she had her first illness, and came to visit from his camp on Telos Lake whenever possible.

This is one of the first cabins built by Al Nugent at his sporting camps. You would probably not go there if you wanted all the comforts of home. Some have called it a semi-wilderness experience. Although Al and Patty are not alive, the camps are still going strong.

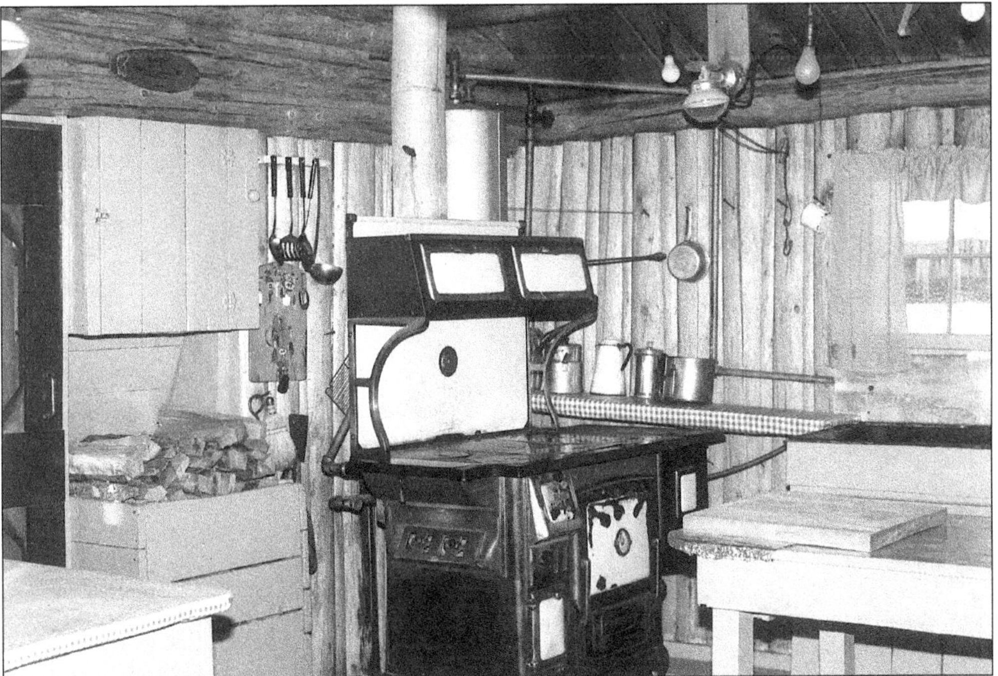

Seen here is the Round Oak wood stove Patty Nugent cooked upon at Nugent's. Patty never blacked it but washed and greased it. Birch and beech plus softwood were the fuel in that stove. There were big heater stoves in the cabins. You did not cook on them until the cabins were eventually put on a housekeeping basis.

Al and Patty Nugent wave goodbye to a plane taking off from Chamberlain Lake by their camps. Al was over six feet tall and weighed 278 pounds at his top weight. Patty was about five foot seven and also weighed 278 pounds at her top. At one time, when she got Bright's disease, she bottomed out at 130 pounds and, when she got well, went up to 180.

Al Nugent is in his element, cooking over a fire deep in the Allagash woods. He guided. He trapped. He hunted and fished. He did all kinds of jobs around his camps and built most of the complex. He was also a well-known storyteller.

Al and Patty pose in their younger years. They are often considered "the love story of the Allagash." Patty was no slouch. She was very strong and said she was all muscle when she weighed 278 pounds. She was a licensed guide for four years, until the camps took up most of her time. She had her own trapping line and hefted 100-pound bags of flour as well as any man.

Al Nugent proudly shows off what is either a land-locked salmon or togue to wife Patty. Patty also was no slouch as a fishing person. She did not like to cook fish very much. Her specialties included corn fritters, doughnuts, pies and other desserts, baked beans (yellow eyes or pea), carrot salad, ham, and potatoes on Saturday nights. She did not usually cook venison or bear meat.

Fred King, who estimated that he guided more than 150 parties around the Allagash, stands at the campsite named after him on Eagle Lake in the Allagash Wilderness Waterway. Standing with him are Mark Chronister, Andy Rubin, Dana Chronister, and Patrick Rubin.

If you go south on the Allagash River, you are likely to have to pole part of the way against the current, as the river runs south to north. Fred King shows how to do it. It is better to have poles with your paddles. You can keep your canoe away from rocks better with a pole than with a paddle. It is a good tool to use in going through rapids.

Fred King demonstrates using a pole while going through rapids on the Allagash. That is a long canoe he is riding in. It looks like there are the remains of a bridge or a dam on either side of the river here. Canoeing the Allagash is not always easy.

Before he had a beard, Fred King is seen preparing a meal beside the Allagash. King did not always get along with state regulations and regulators in the Allagash Wilderness Waterway. He opposed establishment of the waterway. He built tables for several Allagash campsites without state permission. When he got word from a state regulator that the tables might be destroyed, he kept at it and ended up with a campsite named after him.

Fred King eventually built this beautiful camp on Chemquasabamticook (Ross) Lake, west of the Allagash Wilderness Waterway. He named it Camp One-Eye after One-Eye Michaud, a well-known Allagash guide. He had help from the forest ranger at Daaquam on the Maine-Quebec border in getting the first two loads of materials for the camp.

Seen here is Red, Fred King's pet fox, at his camp on Ross Lake. Fred leased the land for his camp from Seven Islands Land Company, one of the large timberland owners in the area. Fred, who worked on engineering surveys of the area as a young man, did not start guiding parties around the Allagash until he was 50 years old.

Fred King stands while members of one of his parties sit in a canoe as they go around the Allagash. Note the motor on the craft Fred was using. The water looks a little low, but the scenery is great. If you like to canoe, the Allagash offers a certain amount of challenge.

Wilfred "Sleepy" Atkins was a game warden, warden supervisor, sporting camp owner, and trapper in the Maine woods for years. He is seen standing on the left and wearing his warden's hat in this 1930s winter photograph. The two men with him are unidentified.

This is one way to hold a bear. Sleepy Atkins, who generally looked down on bear and moose hunters, got this bear. He did not much like bear meat, so he probably did not eat it. The photograph was taken in the 1930s on an island in the Allagash area.

The Allagash area was an excellent place to shoot deer. Sleepy Atkins is on the left, and the other man is unidentified. This image was probably taken when Atkins was operating Atkins' Fishing and Hunting Camps on Millinocket Lake (not the Millinocket Lake near the town of that name).

Atkins' Camps were located west of the tiny town of Oxbow, where he was born, and east of Chamberlain Lake. They were not in what is now the Allagash Wilderness Waterway but were certainly in the Allagash area. It took one day to go from Oxbow to the camps, and a guide took you. The rates were $3 a day for a cabin and board, $4 a day for guide's wages, and $1 a day for a canoe with motor and outfit.

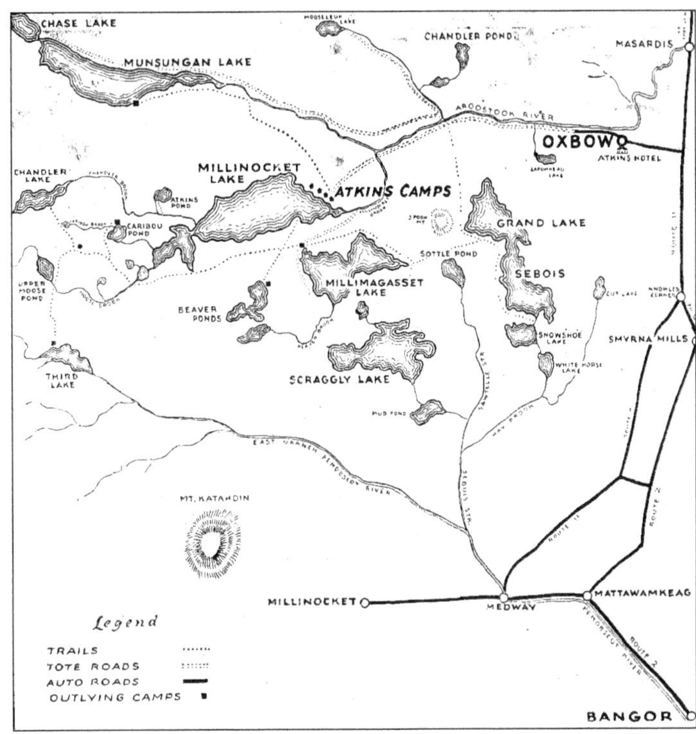

Sleepy Atkins was a fine-looking man in his younger years. The river he is canoeing on is not named, but you can bet it was in the Allagash area. He learned how to oversee a canoe from his father, who owned a chain of sporting camps in the area.

Percy Jackson was born in the town of Allagash, in which the Allagash Wilderness Waterway has its northern end. Raised learning knowledge of the outdoors, he began guiding at the age of 12 in 1923. This image of him was taken when he was 13 or 14 years old.

Percy Jackson, in his prime in the 1930s, does a little log rolling in the midst of a river in the Allagash area. It could have been while he was cutting pulp in the Fox Brooks area. Jackson did not get an actual guide's license until the 1930s.

In this 1957 photograph, Percy Jackson is seen with a horse owned by Guy Kelly in front of one of Kelly's camps. The little girl is Donna Day. The horse standing next to a pick-up truck is symbolic of what happened in the Allagash area when cars took over and logging roads opened the whole territory.

Ira McNally first went around the Allagash in 1914. When he reached his seventies, he was still in the midst of the big woods of northern Maine. He is seen sitting comfortably in his canoe after having gone through a series of rapids. He was, of course, an expert canoeist.

Ira McNally works on a canoe on the shore of Fish Lake, which is east of the Allagash Wilderness Waterway. He had started his career as a cook in lumber camps. The experience stood him in good stead when he guided for sporting camps in the area. Clients raved about his cooking.

McNally (center) holds an eight-and-one-quarter-pound lake trout in May 1966. McNally was 75 years old at the time. Dorothy Robinson is on the right. On the left is Dr. Everett Pierce. McNally remembered the days when you could always catch as many fish as you wished in the Allagash area.

McNally remained active in the northern Maine woods for years. At the age of 80, he was still poling and paddling canoes, this time at Fish Lake. However, note that there is also a motor on the canoe. He looks like he is just about to take off on the lake.

McNally was still going strong in the northern Maine woods at the age of 81. Here, he stands in front of Fish Lake Falls. He died in 1977. He said the greatest shooter he ever saw was Annie Oakley in Ashland *c.* 1905. She was representing the Union Metallic Cartridge Company.

This photograph, taken on Chamberlain Lake in the Allagash, shows Coe and Pingree's old powder house. From left to right are James Hart, Reuben Hart, David Downing, and Henry Averill. Coe and Pingree was a lumbering and logging company. The house stored, among other things, dynamite to break up logjams.

A Connors-Carlson logging crew poses on Churchill Lake, now part of the Allagash Wilderness Waterway. There is a peavey. Most of the men are standing on large logs being pulled by the horses. Second from the right is what appears to be a horse-drawn pung with driver. This appears a standard pose for lumbermen and their horses.

Seven

MORE ON THE ALLAGASH

The words under this photograph say this is part of the Telos Cut (Canal), which diverted water from Chamberlain Lake in the Allagash so logs could go by water to Bangor via the Penobscot River. That use was discontinued *c.* 1920. Most prominent in the photograph is dri-ki on the shore, evidence that the water level had been changed.

Jake McEachern was an old-time dam tender in the Allagash country, mostly at Chamberlain Lake. In *The Wilderness from Chamberlain Farm*, Dean Bennett says McEachern was a great broad axe man. The word was that he would lay 10 matches on a chopping block and swing his axe to clip the match heads, one at a time, just enough to light them.

This old tote road ran from the mouth of Dole Brook to Pittston in the Allagash. Compare this to the paper company roads that festoon much of the Allagash region (back from the river) now. This road would come out far behind. It is also far worse than the Tote Road in Baxter State Park.

The river log drive was exciting. This view shows as well as any just how dangerous log driving could be. The waters of what is now the Allagash Wilderness Waterway and Baxter State Park were once used this way. Three of the men shown are Arthur York, Orville Clark, and Edmond Nadeau. The others are unidentified.

There is plenty of snow in the Allagash River and Baxter State Park region. In the 1890s, there were horse-drawn snowplows like the one seen here. It is not clear from the photograph just where the horse went. The size of the icicles on the shed shows that this photograph was taken near the dead of winter.

The St. John is the river into which the Allagash River flows as its current moves north. A large portion of the area bordering the St. John River was recently purchased by the Nature Conservancy. The fishing is still relatively good. Naturally, the river is much narrower here than after the Allagash and Black Rivers flow into it.

See if you can spot the partridge near the St. John River. Its color blends in with the foliage, a protective device for self-defense, especially against hunters. Even without protective coloring, partridge are pretty hard to shoot. Note the leaning trees in the background.

This photograph shows how low and narrow the St. John River can become in its upper reaches. The man is unidentified. The canoe does not appear able to combat the low water. There is only one thing to do in that case. Unless one is able to pole the canoe, he must carry it.

Chesuncook Village lies at the head of the lake with the same name. This is how it looked on June 29, 1946. Undoubtedly, there are fewer buildings now. The opening of Telos Lake, at the start of the Allagash Wilderness Waterway, to automobile traffic has cut down on the population of the village.

Here, Mike Putnam shows part of what one may have to carry from Chesuncook to Umbazooksus Lake. It is better to be in good shape when you travel there. Putnam, obviously, was in shape.

We see a couple of wharves lying out of the water and several cabins at Umbazooksus Lake. It is doubtful whether any of these still exist. This lake is now off the beaten path on the route to the Allagash because of the road to Telos Lake.

Mike Putnam works on an axe handle at a camp on Eagle Lake, now part of the Allagash Wilderness Waterway. There is a reflector oven beside Putnam. Also in the photograph are the wooden hangers made by Putnam, one holding a frying pan and another a can that probably had coffee in it.

Mike Putnam, long pipe in hand, sits comfortably on the shore of Eagle Lake. Moments like this make all the labor on an Allagash trip worthwhile.

You did not always have to carry your canoes yourself in the Allagash area. Here, Mike Putnam and one of the people he guided, Dr. Kaplan, are on the Umbazooksus horse carry. That horse-drawn carry existed many years. Some said the fee for the horse carry was too much—but there was no other method of going that way.

The trees are still standing but look like they could fall at any moment. Dr. Kaplan is looking them over. Sometimes loggers did not complete their jobs, or they found they did not need the trees they had started cutting. Cutting practices in the 1930s and 1940s were not standardized. This view was at Eagle Lake.

Chase Carry Rips is usually a carry on the ordinary Allagash River trip. Here, however, Mike Putnam is wielding his pole to help him get his canoe through the rapids. The image gives some idea of the wild beauty of what is now the Allagash Wilderness Waterway. The author, on his one trip up the Allagash, had no difficulty with these rapids, though he was an inexperienced canoeist. There were two reasons for this—the water was quite high, and there was an experienced canoeist at the other end of the craft. If you are inexperienced, it is imperative that you have an experienced person with you in the canoe. You might have problems in ordinary places on the river if you do not. Two inexperienced people in a canoe can spell trouble on the Allagash.

Eagle Lake, now part of the Allagash Wilderness Waterway, is seen through a birch tree stand on its shore in the 1930s. The Allagash is scenic from both the water and the shores. It is reminiscent of the birch-lined view of Meduxnekeag (Drew's) Lake in New Limerick, where the author spent many summers.

When the water is low in the Allagash, you have to pole your canoe for best results. Some guides used to clear out rocks and other obstacles so their clients could get through in canoes. Here, Mike Putnam poles on the brook running from Mud Pond to Chamberlain Lake.

This is a catch from Round Pond, now on the Allagash Wilderness Waterway. Former guides in the area say the catch is off from what it was years ago. This photograph was taken in the 1930s. The number of fish caught was 17. It looks like they are on an overturned canoe.

The most dangerous spot on the Allagash River canoe trip, Chase Carry Rips, is made a bit more dangerous by the falls to which it leads and around which you must carry your canoe. There is good scenery around the rips. One problem exists—you are too busy paddling to really notice the scenery.

One of the essences of the Allagash canoe trip is shown in this 1924 photograph. People who did not know one another bond together when they take it. This is an unidentified group on an island in Eagle Lake. Everyone looks happy, and some are horsing around. Unless you have gone around the Allagash with a group whose members you do not know (as the author did on his one trip), you probably would not realize how strong this bonding feeling is after a couple of days. Some relationships established there may last for years. People have a chance to do things on the trip that they never may have done before. The Allagash River experience is a wholly human event.

It is 1930 and this is the dam on Long Lake. There is still a dam at the location and a campsite named for it on the Allagash Wilderness Waterway. The legend on the back of the photograph says, "Beaver House." Since no real beaver house is visible, that must be the name of a building in the background. The evolutionary cycles in an area like the Allagash result in some dilapidation. Buildings are beginning to fall apart. The name Beaver House may be a term of derision for the buildings in the background. A beaver house may be quite solid, but there are usually fragments of logs and bits of wood that stick out on the sides. It was not a compliment to those buildings.

This is the main cabin at Nugent's on Chamberlain Lake not too long after it was built by Al and Patty Nugent. Anywhere else but the Allagash you could be certain it was the dead of winter, but there it could be late fall or early spring.

In this 1919 photograph, Mike Putnam, just back from service in World War I, holds a couple of does that have been shot near Griswold, a mail stop on the Bangor and Aroostook Railroad, east of the Allagash River. Putnam had long service in World War I.

Bill Caldwell, who was a guiding client of Mike Putnam, sits by the fire in 1938. Food is one of the most important ingredients in the usual Allagash trip. Some even supply lobsters the first couple of days. Then you go on to fish, cooked before your eyes after they have been caught. The fresh air and canoeing exertions increase your appetite. If you get sick of fish, there is probably steak around. Also, there are those who sneak in a little venison or moose meat in case of real famine.

Seen in this 1938 photograph is Bill Caldwell at Haymock Lake, which is now just east of the Allagash Wilderness Waterway. Caldwell was a skilled canoeist.

Sometimes dri-ki can get in the way of a canoe. Sometimes, you have to get out and push, as seen in this 1914 photograph near the shore of Chesuncook Lake. The channel was probably pushed out by the two unidentified men. You certainly cannot see Chesuncook Village in this view.

Eventually, Al Nugent built nine cabins at Nugent's on Chamberlain Lake. The ice on the lake may be thick enough for it to be winter. The Nugents always had an ice chisel with them when they traveled and tested the ice thickness with it before they went forward.

Dr. Fred Steele shows off another Allagash fish catch. He caught eight beauties. Obviously, the 1930s photograph was taken in camp, as signs of camp are seen behind Steele.

Seen are the tools of the trade when it came to an Allagash canoe trip years ago. In the reflector oven is a johnny cake. This is on the shore of Allagash Lake. The rocks were available to make a fireplace if they were not already in place at a campsite. It only took a few minutes to set up all this.

Chesuncook Village, from a distant shore of that lake, did not look like much in the 1930s. However, as you got closer to it, the little town loomed large after the Allagash wilderness. When it had its hotel, the village appeared even larger. It was then a jumping-off point for the Allagash.

Mike Putnam (left) and his son Bob take it easy as they fish on the Allagash. Mike allowed his sons to study the outdoors at their own speed. They learned a good deal and also learned to fly to take their father places for hunting and fishing he had never been.

Camps on the Allagash were not always things of beauty. This view was taken on Eagle Lake in the 1930s. However, looks are deceiving in this case. You could have a wonderful time in such a camp—especially if you had a good cook. A good guide could be very helpful.

Another example of an Allagash camp is shown here, on Chamberlain Lake. It looks like some clean-up was necessary when this stay was over. The table seems to have a great deal on it, and the material in the foreground does not seem well organized.

Here is another example of work on the Allagash. Mark Rand is trying to fix a broken pole. That pole seems a bit thin to use as a canoe pole. Maybe it was a tent pole or a clothes pole of some kind. A canoe is in the background, but the exact location is unidentified.

We say goodbye to the Allagash. This 1946 photograph was taken from a Folsom's Flying Service plane from Greenville over Allagash Lake. You could fly to Greenville, Houlton, or nearly anywhere you wished in those days.

Seen here is a duo at the summit of Mount Katahdin in the 1930s. Dr. Kaplan is on the left with Mike Putnam. It is not quite clear what the two are doing up there. Putnam looks like he is reading something. Perhaps it was a list of people who had made the top.

Many have painted Mount Katahdin. Dick Putnam of Granville, Ohio, has painted it after climbing it. Many of his ancestors were greatly involved with the mountain. His painting includes a pond that is probably in the Togue Pond area. The mountain looks beautiful with a snow crown upon it. It is a solemn and peaceful feeling that you get when you look at this painting. Katahdin is a majestic sentinel. It is the mountain where a very young Donn Fendler was lost for 12 days and then emerged from the wilderness. The spirit of the mountain, Pamola, was very kind to Fendler. Katahdin is a symbol of the changelessness of nature.

www.ingramcontent.com/pod-product-compliance
Lightning Source LLC
LaVergne TN
LVHW081529100826
845153LV00004B/239

* 9 7 8 1 5 3 1 6 0 6 2 7 5 *